My Inner Eye
Reflections Seen Through a Veil of Time

Also by Michael F. Lepore

Forgotten Heroes
Poems for and about Veterans of the Vietnam War
(2010)

Vietnam Voices
Echoes of the Vietnam Experience
(2014)

Moral Injury
A Vietnam War Journey of Moral and Spiritual Confusion
(2017)

My Inner Eye
Reflections Seen Through a Veil of Time

poems
Michael F. Lepore

GRAYSON BOOKS
West Hartford, CT
www.GraysonBooks.com

My Inner Eye
Copyright © 2018, Michael F. Lepore
published by Grayson Books
West Hartford, CT
printed in the USA

ISBN: 978-0-9994327-4-7

Interior & Cover Design: Cindy Mercier
Cover Art: "American Coot," cuatrok77 on Visual hunt / CC BY-SA
Author photo courtesy of Bryan Ambrose

for Nancy
my number one critic and number one supporter

All my love!

Contents

I.

Freshness in the Air	11
Spring's Fancy	12
Silver Dollar	13
Morning	15
Carmela Ciccolella	16
Angel of the Morn	18
On Our Own	19
Tension in the Air	21
River Tempest	23
Life's Plan	24
A Path Together	25
A Friend Lost	26
To the Grieving Widow	27
Upon the Stone of Memory	28

II.

First Encounter	33
Coming of the Dawn	35
Autumn's Spell	36
Late Garden	37
The Barn	38
Firebox	39
Theater of Life	40
He's Not Going to Miss Her	41
Wall Clock	43
Mortal Reward	45
Sharing	46
Forever Young	47
Time Together	49
His Mark	50

About the Author   51

I

Freshness in the Air

Crisp brown leaves break free
from earth's frozen hold,
dance, uninhibited, in concert
with brisk breezes
like school children let out for recess.

Warm sun, eager to start the day,
arrives early, lingers long into dusk.
A sense of freshness in the air,
sycamores blush with red hue
of newness, ground colored
in shades of green, dotted specks
of yellow, pink and blue.

Robin returns to greet the worm,
goldfinch dons his vest of yellow,
bluebirds greet the newborn blooms,
air filled with perfume. I breathe deep.
My feet begin to feel spring
in every step.

Spring's Fancy

Nightingale, perched on high,
full-throated treble to a cloudless sky.

Plowshare stands aged, defiant,
where last its mark was made.

Blue Heron glees as winter waters ebb.
Red-tail soars, uninhibited.

Lily-of-the-valley enchants
upon gentle breezes,

awakens within hawthorn sweet memories
of romance in blushes of pink.

Youthful daffodil, body straight and strong,
face sinless, swells with notions of grandeur.

Seeds, like innocent hearts,
sleep beneath their winter blanket,

dream of adventures in fresh spring air.

Silver Dollar

It's Grandpa's birthday—
Aunt Josephine's fried dough,
topped with her special tomato sauce;
peppers, onions, sweet Italian sausage
frying on the outside grill under
watchful eyes of Uncle Sistine.

Bare-foot in the large field with cousins
Raymond, Butchy, and Honeygirl,
staying clear of purple staining berries
that fall from Grandpa's prized mulberry tree,
then, the pause in our activity—

Grandpa sits on a metal kitchen chair
in the center of the lawn—a king
ready to hold court—waits
for his grandchildren to line up
before him. In Italian, he complains
we take too long. Finally my turn,

I stand staring into a face worn
by eighty seven years of toil, head full
of wispy gray hair, a bushy mustache
that no self-respecting Italian grandfather
would be without.

With no words exchanged, he places
in my open palm a silver dollar.

That day is long gone—memories
now tug at the layers of fog that hide
their faces.

The house, still there, smaller than
remembered. The large field, overgrown,
casts gloom over the once idyllic playground.
I stare as if in trance, waking worn, old.
I still have that silver dollar protected
in a ragged Masters cigar box,

along with vintage baseball cards
and prized marble shooters. From time
to time I take out that cherished coin,
clasp it tightly in my palm to remind
myself that it wasn't all just a dream.

Morning

Shadows of bare tree limbs
break free from the darkness,
herald the coming of dawn.

She opens the window, greets
sweet spring air and breathes
fragrances of the chilly morn.

A solitary chirp, as if by magic,
awakens a multitude of golden
notes from a choir of unseen
warbling throats—

wordless melodies in praise of spring
rise in joyful freedom to the sky,
causing it to blush in hues of pink
that wash across the horizon

then melt into the last of the grayness.
First signs of light draw her closer,
her heart captured by the repeated refrains.

She stares out the window beyond
the horizon. What visions does she see,
how far off, how fair?

Carmela Ciccolella

A young man, arms folded
across his chest, obediently
reclines on the kitchen table.
He has been here before.

She stands over him holding
a sprig of lavender in one hand
and a crucifix in the other, waits
to receive the power.

Praying out loud
in her Southern Italian dialect,
she touches his forehead
with the crucifix,

brushes his shoulders
with lavender repeating
her prayers several times,
invoking Saint Michael.

Then she makes the sign
of the cross on his forehead
with olive oil and massages
his head with her thumbs.

After her concluding prayers,
the young man sits up
free from the demons of his head
and the shoulder pain.

She looks at the young couple
sitting in the kitchen
who tensely wait for her magic touch.
She invites them to the table.

Today she is gone, taken away
by time, and the world is not the same
as when she first came.
Although she leaves no monument,

her presence looms large
in bygone afternoon legends.
I feel a closeness.
Her blood runs through my veins.

Angel of the Morn

Daffodils and hyacinths
all greet the morning sun
with excitement and anticipation

They shake the dew from their limbs
and paint their face with sunshine.
They splash on their best perfume
in anticipation of she who is to come.

At once they sense her presence.
Orioles sound the cheer.
She floats with ease among them,
this Muse with auburn hair.

She stops to greet each,
missing not a pair. They rise to meet
her gentle hand. She caresses with a touch
that says she truly cares.

She tucks them in their beds,
gives them nourishing food.
She takes away the worn
and makes them feel like new.

She pauses just a moment
to whistle a chickadee from afar.
They engage in close conversation
like two cronies at a bar.

She continues with nurturing hands
making everything right,
always adding new members
to her chorus of delight.

Then, before she leaves them
she ponders for awhile
till she sees the chosen one.
Her approval is her smile.

On Our Own
the winter of 1963

Plastic reindeer and jolly snowmen
adorn the streetscape. Windows
and doorways are outlined in blinking
colored lights. The small trailer park
heralds the approach of holidays.

Breathing in the festive air, we fire up
the 54 Buick, wrap our legs in towels
to combat bitter cold emerging
from holes in the floorboards, and head
out in search of our first Christmas tree.

A used construction trailer
better suited for Florida living
is our home. The heating unit,
a kerosene stove, sans ductwork,
emits heat directly from the firebox.

The thermometer registers 100 degrees
above that stove, while in the bedroom,
it reads 32 degrees. Ice clings
to the bathroom walls.

We return with our first little tree,
place it in a large juice can filled with dirt
and secure it to the wall with twine
to keep it from falling over.
The tree develops a personality of its own—

adorned with a string of colored lights,
a dozen newly acquired ornaments
and a few vintage balls from her mother.
We string popcorn garlands
and make colored paper link chains.

Nancy makes a cardboard star
I attached to the top of the tree.
As the winter wind howls, buckling the walls.
We huddle together on the floor,

the only illumination, tiny colored lights
and the reflection of a blinking yellow orb
from the shiny special star on top of the tree.
The glow permeates the room with a blanket
of warmth and comfort, cloistering us
from the dark and windy outside.

We sit there all evening, not needing to say a word,
thinking how truly fortunate we are
to have all that we have.

Tension in the Air
spring, 1968

Sidewalks patrolled by uniformed
national guardsmen brandishing
automatic weapons. Curfew required.
All off the streets before 4:30 pm.

That should not pose a problem.
It's Saturday and I'm at the dental school
to take the National Boards to graduate.

Although it is May, the MLK assassination
still hangs heavy in Baltimore and in D.C.
A cloak of distrust and resentment
envelops blacks and whites.

In an effort to beat the curfew, I hurry back
to my car three blocks from the school.
I've parked it in the same spot for four years.

Today no smiling faces greet me.
No waving hands. Mud covers
my little Beetle. Quickly, quietly
I unlock the car, and drive off,

stopping at the trailer park where we live,
midway between the two cities. I wash the Beetle.
After kissing Nancy and the kids, I'm off to work
at the Grand Union store north of the City.

Not long after arriving at work, the ground
begins to shake—an earthquake?
All the employees rush outside.

A convoy of Bradley tanks rumbles down the street,
tearing up the roadbed, making a sharp left turn
on into the northwest quadrant of the City.

Back in the store office, a telephone call
from a co-worker who lives in the city.
He tells me he's on the floor, trapped
in his apartment, won't be able to make it to work.

They're burning my neighborhood!
I hear the panic in his voice, tell him
to be safe and get out as soon as possible.

I never see him again.

River Tempest

The river appears calm now,
apologetic for yesterday's tantrum.
In her wake, disorder.

Dragonfly darts back and forth,
seeks home displaced by nocturnal fury.

Blue Heron retreats to safety
in sheltered glen until morning stars
that cross the sky are mirrored
in placid waters.

Misty veil of dew cloaks a highway
of uprooted hardwood, detached lumber
carried toward an uncertain future downstream.

Slowly, the river loosens her swollen grip,
recedes to former self. Mallards return
to the comfort of her bed, quacking
and gossiping again.

Primeval melodies stir her restless spirit,
confined within glacial banks
yet free to follow her path.
Lure of the deep sea draws her onward.

Life's Plan

It will lead you to the top
of the mountain. It will plunge
you into the depths of the dark.

It will embrace your longing soul,
fill your heart with joy, while thorns,
obscured by the beauty of the rose,
may cause you pain.

It will bid you to follow faithfully
in your true desires, even though the way
may be rough and unsure.

It will speak to you in confidence.
It will demand an attentive ear,
though its words may shatter
your hopes and aspirations.

Life will shape you, it will guide you
in your growth, so that you may appreciate
the complexity of its plan.

A Path Together

Let us pause here and dream
while the clear morning sunlight
on the moist young grass,
and the trees, newly clothed in green,
guide our thoughts to some remote,
sweet corner of the soul.

Let us walk silently, arm in arm,
in close companionship,
with no speech between us, save
the language of an understanding heart,
as the path becomes long.

Let us breathe in the sweet summer air,
and hear, a robin's song of youth.
Although this loveliness will begin to fade,
let us hold each other and reflect
upon the promises we kept.

Let us cherish the warmth we share,
and ponder the effects of our achievements,
more clearly seen each day upon this path.
Let us vow, within our secret soul,
to make beauty our greatest goal.

A Friend Lost

I sit in a room that is strangely
still, lingering hint of stale roses.
Accolades and prayers now forsaken,
replaced with sorrowful thoughts.

I sort through complex feelings,
The words I never said,
unnecessary to share during
the years of good times.

We kept each other close—work, play
and travel. It was hard to keep pace,
tennis before work, fishing in Belize,
antiquing in Vermont and the Vineyard.

How could a seemingly healthy man,
who never smoked, end up with
a double lung transplant? For six years
he battled, with dignity,
the formidable dragon of time.

We got together, his blood pressure
so low he could not walk from one room
to the next without stopping to rest
in a chair. He was going to Boston in a
couple of days to get that checked.

He took a turn for the worse,
an infection that spread, a fever
that would not leave. One could ask
only so much.

He fought long and hard, always
with a smile, only to have the limits
of his body betray him.
I always thought that I would see him again.

To the Grieving Widow
With inspiration from "The Prophet" by Kahlil Gibran

For what is it to cease breathing,
but to free the soul from its restless
tides so it may soar and seek God
unencumbered. For what is it to die
but to stand naked in the wind and
to melt into the sun.

That which you love in him most
is clearer in his absence.
In your sorrow, look into your heart
and you shall see that you are weeping
for that which has brought you joy.

Only by experiencing sorrow can joy
be recognized. Together they come,
and when one sits alone with you
at the table, remember that the other
is asleep upon your bed. Search for
the secret of death in the heart of life,
for they are one, even as the river
and the sea are one.

Upon the Stone of Memory

Upon the stone of memory I shall stand,
await the sunrise kiss, sigh at the warrior's song,
and retrace echoing footsteps walked hand in hand.

Youthful hearts strive to discover firsthand
how a cause so great could do so much wrong.
Upon the stone of memory I shall stand.

Deep-rooted truths shine like castles in the sand.
Some goals unreachable, but still I go along
and retrace echoing footsteps walked hand in hand.

How hope and love ward off defeat and
yet by some mysterious grace remain strong.
Upon the stone of memory I shall stand.

Within my heart a fire burns to understand
more clearly the beauty of wisdom's song,
and retrace echoing footsteps walked hand in hand.

When Age has laid its hand as planned,
and I retrace my steps walked yearlong,
upon the stone of memory I shall stand,
and retrace echoing footsteps walked hand in hand.

II

First Encounter

All the good seats were taken.
I managed to find one somewhat close
to the front. I heard this poet was worth
the trip; knowledgeable, entertaining,
well published.

I concentrated on his lips,
how they mouthed each word,
made certain not to miss one syllable.
Soon his monotonous tone strained
my attention. His voice fainter,
my mind began to wander.

I searched the room for something,
anything to rescue me from impending
slumber. Then, as if by divine intervention,
I found a most intriguing pair of legs.

My interest focused on the firmness
of her thighs as they met her knee,
the gentle curve of her calf, the arch
of her well sculpted foot, shoe sensually
dangled from painted toes – far more
interesting than anything he could say.

He read his poems of global warming,
economic crisis or something like that.
My thoughts were on those legs, how
they would feel wrapped around my waist.

I felt the urge to loosen my collar as a wave
of heat flushed my face. I stretched my neck
to discover those legs belonged to the poet's wife.
Her stoic face shared my boredom.

Bedroom eyes relegated to counting ceiling tiles,
soothing fingers massaging a set of lucky car keys;
I could write poems about her. I'm sure he will too,
after she leaves him, perhaps for another poet,
the quiet and attentive type, the type that truly
appreciates the beauty in her lines.

Coming of the Dawn

The ceremony ended,
my benediction delivered, I begin
to make my way through small groups
of well-wishers looking to exit.

A bright face blocks my path,
There is something strangely familiar
about her, like a friendly ghost
uneager to depart.

She begins to praise my work
in a voice almost familiar.
Do I know her? She is well-dressed
and her appearance craves my attention.

While she speaks I examine her face
and try to recall where I've met her before.
Her manner calm, not setting herself apart.
I know those eyes,

bolder than I last remembered, belonging
to someone who has walked a hard path
out of the dark, into the dawn.

Ray, is that you? She responds,
Call me Alice.

Autumn's Spell

Humid haze that causes katydids
to stir succumbs to cool breezes.
Songs of summer, light and carefree,
wane as warming sun becomes brief
in an icy sky.

Gnarly quince hangs untouched,
yellow and full, Aphrodite's golden
apple, waiting to charm the hearts
of brides and grooms. Its captivating
essence promises sweet affection.

Mourning Dove bemoans last breath
of the sunflower. Sweet nectar of aster
warns honey bees these days will not last.
Mature leaves twist and turn,
break free, head homeward to their roots.

Late Garden

Squirrels are darting here
and there, still gathering,
still building.

Unique forms and fancies
that caring hands have coaxed
still brighten the garden,
though this loveliness will fade.

The fallen petals will be tinged
with brown, the proud sunflower
will bend its head to the ground.

The wind breathes a chilling sigh.
One by one lost leaves
fall to the ground, rustle about,
then become silent among the gloom.

Still we tend the soil, staying true to the plan,
tend to the duties that we must, vow to speak
words we should have long since said.

Among the decay and faint sweet odor
of wilted flowers, high in the dark shadows
of the magnolia tree a chorus of tiny,
throbbing throats sing songs of youth.

Within my heart a coldness flows.
It is I who have grown old.

The Barn

Like a sentinel of a more graceful day
it stands strong, defiant against the winds
of a harsher climate—of winter cold and rain,
of summer sun beating down
on a roof of cracking slate.

In its younger day it provided strength
and purpose for those entrusted to its care.
Now it's just a home to mice to run and play,
and for a few chipmunks that wander
in and out throughout the day.

Who is left to sing its song, to tell the tales
of what it's seen? Like the chill December night
when our calf, Bailey, was born
and Nancy cradled her like a baby
into the early morn.

We read the past on silent walls
where words and numbers were scrawled
by hired hands writing notes
to say that they were here, or list
the work hours, the wages owed.

Its hallowed halls seem empty now
except when the bitter wind begins to howl.
Then the keening turns to an old music
that listening hearts can hear, a sound
of cowbells as the herd comes wandering in
to fill the milk cans.

Younger feet now pass it by oblivious
to the secrets it could tell. Still it stands
with head held high in hopes that a newer
generation will stop and ask but why.

The Firebox

Outside, white flakes dance
with beads of ice, lofty evergreens
curtsy to howling wind.

Inside, frosty calmness, empty stalls,
memories too cold to speak
held tight in winter's trance.

The small woodstove glistens
in late day light. With a strike
of a match the firebox awakens,
defrosts recollections of days long past.

Sweet smell of warmth stirs barn spider
from its dreams in the rafter above,
instinctively plies the art of the web.

A specter of forgotten years stands
within the shadows, shrouded in a timeless
veil. Her presence chills the warmth,
the stove moans, fiery logs shift,
with a jolt, brawny fibers succumb to embers.

Barn spider hurriedly sets final touches
on her masterly design, scurries
to the sanctuary of the nest.

Specter, indifferent to the blood and tears
that fell the thickest during years of toil,
steps silently into the light;
the stove stares back darkly.

Theater of Life

Upon this stage a drama unfolds,
the story of youth that in time becomes old.

From phlox to pinks the winged servants
comply. No strangers to this dance,
they follow a script written long time past,
future of the garden secure in their grasp.

Pollen, powder of life entrusted to their keep,
Rose, poppy and foxglove take the lead
on a stage alive with activity and color,
each brighter than the next, competing with each other.

Heat of the day begins to wane,
cool north wind brings chilling rain.
Royal mantles tinged with brown,
once-young blooms begin to wear,
color fading—a chill in the air.

Proud heads bent to the ground,
a curtain of darkness descends upon all
with a sense of fulfillment, the final call.

What of Man who thinks himself best,
does arrogance keep him apart from the rest?
Has his time in the garden meant nothing at all,
reluctant to share a script with those destined to fall?

He's Not Going to Miss Her

He sits on the side of the bed,
stares down at a pair of brown shoes,
laces worn, toes scuffed—wonders
who would leave their shoes by his bed?

A knock on the door shifts
his attention—an attractive
young woman, auburn hair
in tasteful disarray, soft hazel eyes—
maybe she is here for the shoes.

Eyes moist, she forces a smile,
kisses the top of his head,
sits in the chair opposite his bed,

*Would you like to hear more
of Treasure Island?*
He answers with a half-smile.
She opens the book, heavier
in her hand with each visit, begins
to read aloud—her voice tugs
at strings that bind his memory.

Drawn to the reflection
in the wall mirror, he stares
at the image peering back—
gray, wrinkled, unfamiliar,
except for the hazel eyes.

Her words stir fading reflections
that pass like tides. She looks up,
hazel eyes searching, in vain.
Drawn to her, he reaches out,
there is something about her eyes.

Afternoon chimes herald an end
to visitation, *I'll see you tomorrow,
Dad,* she kisses the top of his head,
scans his face for signs of recognition.
Maybe tomorrow.

The door closes with a click that
never changes. He stares for a long
moment, puzzled, looks down at a pair
of brown shoes, laces worn, toes scuffed—
wonders who would leave their shoes by his bed.

Wall Clock

His wingback chair is positioned strategically
between the bed and the window
to give a view of his prized vegetable garden,
but his eyes are fixed on the clock
ticking on the wall.

In his prime, he was master
of the house, now an antique fixture
in a one room world surrounded
by fading photographs and a religious statue
holding a pair of dusty rosary beads
sitting on the aged dresser.

His old smoking companion, Prince Albert,
rests on the windowsill, listens to stories,
complaints, passes no judgment.
On the bed, just within arm's length,
in neat order, his favorite pipe, one box
of safety-tip matches and a small pile of coins.

He shifts his eyes from the wall clock
to the mirror attached to the dresser.
Within the depths of its dark surface,
a vision of tender youth, a flame-touched
spirit of beauty, that parted from him
all too early.

His red-rimmed eyes follow images
of love-filled dreams, shadows of lost days.
Many times he shouted for her to stay
but the mirror's cloudiness swept her away.
Today, he feels the warmth of her hand in his.

A youthful glow bathes his face.
He checks the wall clock to make certain
the time is right, gently raises his arms
toward the mirror, opens both hands as if
to receive a precious gift.

A bright, white light washes the room,
cleansing everything in sight. In seconds
the light is gone leaving an emptiness,
a comforting peacefulness.
The wall clock no longer ticks.

Mortal Reward

Day after day, we tread
the same worn path. One
by one our pleasures pass,
our once high held dreams
dissolve to dust.

We continue to do the duties
we must, try, as best we can,
to hide the fatal changes
wrought by time.

When age has laid its hand upon
the heart, and good friends begin
to forever part, we look at joy
and sorrow with the same degree
of trepidation.

Beyond the hedges and gated trellis
a garden dwells, a cloister
against gloom and despair—
pansies with smiling faces, daisies
gently lifting their heads, and regal daffodils
from whose trumpets appear workers
with powdered wings.

Why should the ends to which
we strive be set beyond the boundaries
of mortal life? Is not man made
to enjoy happiness on earth,
why else would a good God give us birth?

Sharing

Not so long ago a girl
with sunlight in her hair
and paradise in her eyes
caressed my hand, and
promised to share a life.

The world was younger than today.
We did not look to the fading
of the flowers, had no need
to question all the answers.

Our hope and determination
fired like a voice from the height
of future years, shaping our path
day by day.

Now we sit in the early morning light
staring into the fireplace. Soft,
warm dancing flames cause us
to ruminate over the past fifty plus years.

Our memory, a woven tapestry
with many threads of various hues,
brighter than sunshine, stronger than moonlight.
We still find satisfaction in this pilgrimage.

She leans her head on my shoulder,
gently caresses the back of my hand
and promises to share a life.

Forever Young

The house seems strangely quiet
in the middle of the day.
It seems that everyone has gone
their separate way.

A chance to spend some time alone
a feeling somewhat new,
although I look forward to it
I'm not quite sure what to do.

I retire to the library
by the fire warm and bright,
ponder over Dante or Milton
to accompany me into the night.

Comfortable in my easy chair
deciding whether to read or nap,
I have this sweet sensation
there's someone at my back.

Quickly they are upon me.
They climb all over my chair,
smother me with kisses,
mess up what's left of my hair.

They are so quick and nimble,
their eyes so clear and bright.
Their giggles are contagious,
they are my day's delight.

They lie across my lap,
tug about my limbs.
They use my legs for chute-the-chute.
I become their jungle-gym.

These days of frolicking are all too short,
that's just how it has to be.
Soon they will have great heights to conquer,
there'll be little time for me.

No matter where life takes them,
how far we are apart,
I'll always keep a part of them
locked tightly in my heart.

Time Together

Treasures held tight in the heart,
that which we think, feel and see,
are but fast fading pictures
on the screen of memory.

Sweetly still we recall those days
that seem not long ago, of the dreams
we shared, being young and wise,
and the goals once glorious in our eyes.

What changes have been brought,
how many hours we have spent
toiling with our hopes and aspirations,
grateful for that which time has lent.

Through cycles and seasons, sunshine
and darkness, your smile, the dearest prize,
lights my face, spreads warmth
like a fire when it is cold outside.

His Mark

Do not dwell on this spot and cry,
it is a journey we all must make.
He is not here, he has not died.

Think of him with head held high,
even though old memories will ache.
Do not dwell on this spot and cry

Now his soul is free to fly.
Earthly remains loose upon the lake.
He is not here, he has not died.

He is the summer breeze that passes by,
the diamond sparkles upon the wake.
Do not dwell on this spot and cry

He is soft stars that shine in evening sky,
the rush of singing birds at daybreak.
He is not here, he has not died.

His voice heard in the rustle of the rye.
His mark enlightening the paths we take.
Do not dwell on this spot and cry,
he is not here, he has not died.

About the Author

Michael Lepore, a retired orthodontist lives with his wife, Nancy, in Glastonbury, Connecticut. They have converted their 1850 Georgian Revival home into a bed and breakfast inn, *A Cardinal House*, where they specialize in small weddings, elopements and the renewal of marriage vows. Upon graduation from the University of Maryland, Baltimore College of Dental Surgery, Lepore received a commission in the U.S. Navy Dental Corps and served his active duty attached to Headquarters, 2nd Marine Division at Camp Lejeune, N.C. 1968 – 1970. He is chaplain and treasurer of the local Veterans' Service Commission and paymaster of the Peter P. Monaco, Jr. Detachment of the Marine Corps League.

Dr. Lepore is the author of *Forgotten Heroes: Poems for and about Veterans of the Vietnam War*, as well as *Vietnam Voices: Echoes of the Vietnam Experience*, and *Moral Injury: A Vietnam War Journey of Moral and Spiritual Confusion*, all published by Grayson Books. His poetry has been featured in numerous journals and collections. His third book, *Moral Injury*, received the Gold Medal Award from the *Military Writers Society of America* in 2017.

www.ingramcontent.com/pod-product-compliance
Lightning Source LLC
Chambersburg PA
CBHW070441010526
44118CB00014B/2146